LUNA BOUND

BOUND TO MOON

KP THIARA

Dedicated to "all those who got healed with my help and also helped me to heal"

Luna Bounded

Bounded to Moon

KP Thiara

Contents

Contents

Foreword

KP Thiara wrote the forward for this poetry book on self empowerment and learn to live life freely and boldly :

> "*When people tell you a story about an incident in their life, it is because they want to unburden themselves. To feel lighter of the things that weigh them down. To feel their problems like gas balloons.*"

> "*When someone has the courage to tell you their story, it will not be easy for them. You don't have to understand what they are trying to tell you. You don't have to wonder what to tell them. All you have to do is to listen.*"

The major theme of the book is *"to be a good listener"* but always remember that *"sometimes a listener too needs a listener"*...

Preface

This book is being written by an Indian Poet, Writer, Singer and a Music Producer Khushpreet Singh Thiara Better known as KP Thiara. This book contains the poetries describing the pain that you feel when you are attached to something from deep of your Heart and suddenly something happens in between you both that causes seperation. Their is a very beautiful reason behind choosing "LUNA" (Moon) as the main theme of the book and naming it "Luna Bounded" which you will get to know after reading the whole book.

> "*Talking to someone for hours is so dangerous*
> *because one day you both will stop talking and it will hurt so much....*
> *- unknown*"

It took KP three months to complete this poetry book, KP has been published thrice as a Punjabi/Panjabi poet and won Amazon Pen to publish Twice. But first time, he is trying the English Poetry.

We hope you will show same love and support to this new era of the blooming poet and writer KP Thiara..

Regards

Team INTER$TELLAR (KHUSH CREATIONS) INC.

Acknowledgements

In this book project i was all alone, but throughout the project but throughout my writing journey many people helped me. First of all I wanna start with my biggest blessing I wanna thank My grandpa Late Mr. Piara Singh Ji who always believed that i can do something bigger in my life.

Secondly I wanna thank all of my other family members who always supported me in my every step at every place. Right now whatever I am its just because of their blessings, support and belief.

Next comes my School teachers at My school St. Soldier Divine Public School, Naya Nangal. who have always guided in right direction and helped me alot, also in acedemics but along with that also in following my passion of writing.

Last but not the least i wanna thank all the lovely creatures that are always about my side. Yeah, You guessed it righyt i wanna thank all my friends. actually they are the ones who supported my writings and encouraged and motevated me to write.

Along with this i wanna thank each and everyone who have been the prt of my this journey.

Thanks to all, Regards

KP Thiara.

Prologue

This book is specially for those who have ever felt so attached to anything...

> "*When you cutoff someone from your life,*
> *they will never tell the full story,*
> *they will only tell them the part that makes*
> *you look bad and them innocent...*
> *- unknown*"

enjoy reading, hope you will like it....

1. Sultan Bahu

I wanna start with some precious wordings of "Sultan Bahu ji"

> *"Master of Masters! Listen to my plaint:*
> *Whome else shallI adress?*
> *To me there is no other like you;*
> *To me there are Millions like me.*
> *Read not my scroll of Evil deeds,*
> *Shut not your soul on this wretched soul*
> *Had I not been steeped in sin, says Bahu,*
> *On whom would you have showered your mercy?"*

- Sultan Bahu

2. Life

Life. Oh. Life
It is meant to be lived
As I bathe in its strife
The way wind works
I feel the breeze And understand with a sense of ease
Oh. Life. Please What sort of place is this?
Consciousness...
Be a friend. A foe. Or maybe even less.
Which way will you go? As I set and travel and traverse
This wide and spacious universe
A few pennies in a purse So I can travel on the beyond
Sing songs with those who are gone
It's in their eyes. Life has said so long
But death be not the end.
The rope holds out so strong.
So, I dangle... Above the rest
Effortlessly, my feet kick
As passion empties from this chest
They say life is a test.
Surely who is the maker?
As life I love... it won't linger.
In new things, a wetness and it's wringer,
To dry out under the chaos

As the things all of it has entered in us..
-KP Thiara

3. Espresso

I dream in a coffee
ice in between my teeth
it sets me free.
Caffeine on my brain
Waiting for the day
Sunshines; no rain
I'm here to stay
till there ain't no more pain.
How are you?
Come find the faith
in the way it hits
and I'm running
and following it.
Espresso and I just
don't know where to go
sit and stay jouney
and let it all be.
Starting the day; I wake up in coffee
Encoumbered as I lay; sipping so softly
I am okay and I am free.
-KP Thiara

4. Pen in My Hand

I'm here to make history
not for you but for me
To die with a smile
and a pen in my hand
I don't expect them to understand
the way it creeps into my soul
like a little tug and a pull
I look to the universe and see it whole
But the every atom and molecule set me free
As the trees blow in soft breeze
Sand shifts under my feet as I run to the ocean
After walking for years on concrete
and my popsicles then melts in the heat
And I smile in the face of my old friend
As she extends her hand I wink at defeat
She knows my means and my heart
and she ain't evil just like death
She comes to let off the hope Weghing Down my shoulders
She says life Could be colder
If I kept going and going; digging pointless holes
So I Got up and Collected my Soul
At Last Oh, well!
I'll See all of them in hell..

5. This is Hell

Casualities
Like opem waves
Played by the seas Floating
Bodies
Come and See
S.T.A.Y and may never leave
This is hell
And you're just a well
Here or there
where the art though?
I know I'll never know
Your graves
I'll never set foot on
You'll Never See me face
So I S.T.A.Y
And walk slow at this pace
Bodies
Come and see
And never leave
This is hell
It's all as well
The way and stories they tell.
Broken and may be stolen

And Maybe still I'm fallen
So, where did I go?
Hey! listen, did you think of me
when you decided to cut-off and leave
making me ask myself and sky
about why...
Visit me in my dreams
I forgive you but still I'm angry
You left me and many others so...
Bodies Come and See
And never leave..
-KP Thiara

6. if I loved you

if I loved you
you would never know
I'd just pack my bags
get up and go.
no need to stay
for the broken heart
and the games you play
so, restless in your skin
you'd like to feel good
but you love to sin
it's all good.
Fir all is fair
In love and war
But what are u here for?
just leave me alone
so I don't have to
block u on my phone...
-KP Thiara

7. I turned 18 this year

"Wrote this on 22nd Jan 2022 (My birthday)"

So much I didn't know about life
learning from mistakes I made
I tried my best to made them happy
and forgot mine, guess I just lied to myself
afraid if they would see me as a evil
didn't fully brave to be who I am.
I let them wrote my story
told me this and that
should be this and that
I was a little guy until 17,
but months ago I made huge decisions
made changes that shocked many
told my desire and what would I be.
today I am 18
I feel like I born again
I feel my journey begins again
I write my own story and ready to experience unknowns
Today, I am 18
I forgive myself for wasn't being whole
I forgive myself for mistakes I made

I forgive myself for wasn't honest
I forgive myself for feeling not enough
I forgive myself for letting them
wrote my life story to made them happy
today I am 18, I born again
I begin again, my journey,
my story, my experience.
good and bad, battles after battles
I am ready to face tomorrow's unborn
I will find my way to come back
to the place where my heart belongs.
I do believe in every mistake
it only shapes me into who I am
a real human being who has flaws
but embrace every evil child in him.
I do believe that it only makes me grow
and to seek more connection
my soul craves in
spirituality and emotionally.
Today I am 18.
-KP Thiara

8. It Wasn't meant to be

Sometimes it doesn't work out, it just doesn't. No matter how hard you try to glue your hearts together, no matter how hard you try to fix it, and no matter how much you talk about the sticky stuff, the painful stuff, the hard, messy, hurts-to-remember-stuff, you can't move on from it. You can't forget the hurt that they caused and how lonely they made you feel every single time that they put you last. You can't forget the expectations you had and how they let you down, time and time again. You can't go back to the gentle, simmering love you had for them when you first met because now, that feeling has been replaced with disappointment, with regret, with wishing that things hadn't gone this way but knowing that you can't go back in time. Because now, too much has happened and you've both said things that you can't take back. Because now, you've seen a side to them that you never knew existed and they've seen a side to you that you didn't know you had the mean, cruel side that only their presence has brought out. Sometimes it doesn't work out because you not only bring the best out in each other but the worst too. And the worst part is knowing that they could have been your forever if only things hadn't gone the way they have. And knowing that even though every part of you wants to hold on to them, you still have to let them go because deep down you know that it just wasn't meant to be

9. Meant to be little Broken

Maybe we're meant to stay a little broken, a little incomplete, and a little imperfect so there's room for growth, so there's room for people to pour their love, their lessons and their warmth into us and make us feel whole again, even if it's for a little while. Maybe we're not meant to heal completely from things and, just like a river, a small ripple of pain or happiness in our lives is supposed to keep us going a long way. Maybe that's what it is. Maybe life isn't about 'winning' or 'losing' but gaining experiences, love, relationships, a family. I know that I want everything figured out. I hate the uncertainty of the path ahead. I get uncomfortable when I think about how blurry my future is. But the best experiences in life are had outside of our comfort zone. Maybe that's what I've gotten wrong this whole time. I shouldn't look at life as a journey for betterment but a journey for growth, whatever that looks like. Maybe that's when I'll be able to say that I'm okay and feel it too.

10. Letting Go

Letting go isn't always about putting the other person in a mental box of people I no longer care about', or blocking them on social media and deleting their number. Letting go isn't always about hating the other person or thinking ill of them. Sometimes, letting go is forgiving them. Letting go is accepting that they hurt you, but refusing to allow that pain to define your entire relationship/friendship, or cloud your memories of them. Letting go is about understanding that sometimes you can love someone and still be disappointed in them, sometimes you can love someone and still distance yourself from them. Sometimes you can love someone but know that because they didn't treat you well, you have to cut off your tics with them. Sometimes you can love someone but still can't forget what they did to you, and that's why you have to leave. Letting go doesn't always mean having negative feelings towards them by the end of it. Letting go can also mean wishing them well and wanting them to bet happy in all their future chapters, but knowing that this last chapter was as far as you both were meant to go. Letting go means keeping them in your heart forever, and moving forward in your life with that feeling, instead of with them by your side.

11. Crossing Path

Some people are only meant to cross paths with you that is all. They are not supposed to stay in your life forever. Some people slip into your life like a rainbow but leave a tornado in their wake making you doubt love and all the good in your life. Making you question whether they truly had to leave, because if they did then why did it feel so wrong? Why did it hurt so much? Because if they had to leave then why did they come into your life to begin with? But they had to. Believe me. Some people are passers-by in a journey that is all about your growth, healing and happiness. These people arrive in the form of daylight and warmth but leave as hard lessons that you stumble over. These people tuck love into the pleats of your heart but leave fragments of themselves behind. These people teach you how to laugh with your eyes closed and they show you in the truest sense- what it means to let love in. But some people are just a stage in your life. An experience. A temporary fixture. A fleeting moment that won't last forever. And these people, these very soulmates who you would do anything for, teach you that no matter how much you care for each other sometimes those you love have to leave, and you have to let them.

12. Wait fo It

Wait for a love that arrives when you least expect it. Love that shows up at your doorstep on a cold wintry evening. Love that takes your hand and presses it against their chest until you can feel their heartbeat. Wait for a love that respects you. Love that doesn't make you second-guess yourself. Love that challenges you to be a better version of yourself. Love that believes in you. Wait for a love that is here for the long run. Love that understands the words commitment' and 'companionship' and doesn't make excuses for their mistakes. Love that trusts you and tries its best to understand your emotions. Wait for a love that is gentle with your heart. Love that brushes delicate fingers over a hand that has been let go of more than once. Love that knows how much you have gone through to find them. Wait for a love that is there through the difficult days. The messy days. The hard-to-forget days. The days when you are at your worst. And the days that are drunk on laughter and happiness. Wait for a love that holds your hand through it all, to steady you. To calm your pattering heart. Love that understands how hard it is having a soft soul in a world that constantly pushes you to be hard. Love that doesn't try to change you in anyway. Wait for a love that stays. A love that stays.

13. I'm Tired

I am so tired of being strong. I‘m so tired of saying that it’s okay every time someone treats me badly. I’m tired of being the bigger person and always making excuses for other people. I'm tired of constantly proving how much people mean to me when they won’t do the same. It’s difficult, isn’t it? Having a big heart, and the ability to forgive so quickly and easily, being the one that always tries their very best to make others happy. And still getting hurt, getting taken for granted and being left behind as though you didn’t mean anything. That’s the thing about being a good person you give yourself so many excuses to look out for others that you forget to look out for yourself. And in the end, when they get everything that they wanted, and they start to walk away without looking back in your direction - you are the one who’s left with a hole in your chest where your heart should have been.

14. It was about them

It was never about finding someone 'perfect'. It was about finding someone who could love you entirely. Someone who may not have had the kind of life that you did -speckled with pain and ounces of heartache but tried their best to understand your journey, your trauma, and your burden. It wasn't about finding someone who 'accepted' you, no. It was about finding someone who saw how magnificent you are. Flawed, yes, but filled with enough love that it could drown them. But they learned to float. Heck, they even learned to swim inside your overwhelming heart. They learned about your scars and internal troubles. They cherished the battles you won. They rooted for you. They wanted you to be happy. It was never about finding someone who didn't judge you for your past. It was about finding someone who acknowledged every experience you've ever had because it made you, you. It was never about finding someone 'perfect'. It was about finding your person. The one whose hand you'd hold at the end of it all and say, 'You don't know how much I've gone through just to be here', and knowing undoubtedly that they understood.

15. A Poet's job

They say a poets job
Is to convey the sublime
Have I done that yet?
Grabbed your attention
With talking about the sunset
But what about what you think.
And what's going on behind
Those eyes that see the words I write
As I palpitate and wait
It's half past eight.
The thought of life escapes.
Water the cool way I breathe
Warm up my fingers
I look at my sheets
and there's a crease
Flatten it and other appears
And I hate crying around all this fear
It's gonna stay. It's gonna be here
But what else can I do
But listen to the waves of yesterday
And all of tomorrow too?
-KP Thiara

16. Sweet Escape

The sweet escape
To the soft crevices of my mind
Velvet flowers
Sitting in this for hours
The power
In the Way I stay and never sour
I'm home
In my heart
And soul
What more
Is there?
This is what
My life is for
Judge me
Persephone
Capture me
And I'd wilt the world
Free me and watch
The skies I fade into
And we both can turn
That brilliant shade of blue.
-KP Thiara

17. You're the wet Metal

The words in truth
I need no rhythm
To find God
I know him
With no hymn
I know her
In all of this water
Gave birth to
The sound of a million
Stars colliding
Into an abyss of energy
Why are you staring
From dust to dust
What kind of life
To never give up lust
In this way am the oxygen
You're the wet metal I rust
-KP Thiara

18. It's Okay

It's ok.
I admitted to a stranger
Yeah. Children would be nice
Better not think twice
Desires in my heart
As I wanna to tear them apart
Crying over what I felt like I can't have
But it's ok. Keep going.
With the whole world at play
I will seek destiny
Let it settle on my soul
Everything and everyone
Is out of my control
Let the fox eat the squirrel
I will remember when I was just a hair curl
No wolf or dog can hold that back
I am forging my way forward
There's a sense of a chrysalis
Left behind. The pain
Need to know bliss
I am changing and evolving
Keep up or stay in your own head
I will fly to the sky

And be the best I can be till I'm dead
-KP Thiara

19. This Thing

This thing that we're doing
It's not true nor false
It's neither a dream or reality
This thing that we feel is undefined, chaotic
This that exist
Only in secret,
Only between us
Only in the smallest, darkest hours
This thing that I wish should never come to an end
But also I wish had never begun
This thing makes me want to define,
Define myself,
Call it yours,
I want to shout syour name,
I want to hear you do the same.
This thing is currently,
Holding my sanity
In the palm of its hands
And I'm watching it filter
Through it's fingers; like sand
this thing, This thing is it...
-KP Thiara

20. Time

The message comes with time.
Time will always be a surprise
If you think the truth is a lie,
look up to the sky
and see that the pain is still alive.
Maybe you don't see it,
or maybe you just want to deny the fact that
it won't have much of an impact.
Nothing seems impossible,
and the mystery will not remain unsolvable.
Beneath the layers of myster
lies colors of truth,
one that reveals itself when you don't want it to.
Do not run off,
to water the seeds of fear that comes with it,
face it now before its unbreakable like a giant sequoia.
Where the truth, is where you find your reflection
so explore the hidden with every passing oscillation.
-KP Thiara

Ending Notes

If I ever Decide to Give up on You

You need to understand how much it took out of me
I'm the type of person who gives endless chances,
Always has your back,
and truely accept you for who you are
when rest of the world didn't want you
I did....
So if I ever decide to give up on you
please understand that it took everything that was left,
inside of me.
To leave you alone....

About The Author

KP THIARA

Khushpreet Singh Thiara better known as KP Thiara is am Indian Poet and record producer. Born on 22nd January, 2004 in Ludhiana, Punjab, India. And Lives in Nangal, Punjab, India. Have completed his 12th from St. Soldier Divine Public School, Naya Nangal. KP Thiara has written more than 3000 poetries and is published thrice as a Hindi and Punjabi poet in books ; Unmad Tera, Bōhara, Sadhraan. And has won Amazon Kindle pen to publish for his work in Bōhara.

Author's Social

KP Thiara's social

instagram : @kp_thiara

indeed : KP Thiara

e-mail : thiarakp@gmail.com

youtQuote : kp_thiara

Spotify / Apple Music : Imter$tellar

9 798887 720319

Printed by Libri Plureos GmbH in Hamburg,
Germany